THE
ROSE

MetroBooks

MetroBooks

An Imprint of the Michael Friedman Publishing Group, Inc.

First MetroBooks Edition 2002
©2000 by Michael Friedman Publishing Group, Inc.

ISBN 1-58663-549-2

Editor: Susan Lauzau
Art Director: Jeff Batzli
Designer: Jennifer Markson
Photography Editor: Wendy Missan
Production Managers: Camille Lee and Leslie Wong

Color separations by Colourscan Co Pte Ltd
Printed in Singapore by CS GRAPHICS, Pte, Ltd.

1 3 5 7 9 10 8 6 4 2
For bulk purchases and special sales, please contact:
Michael Friedman Publishing Group, Inc.
Attention: Sales Department
230 Fifth Avenue
New York, NY 10001
212/685-6610 FAX 212/685-3916

Visit our website:
www.metrobooks.com

INTRODUCTION

More than any other flower, the rose has laid claim to the human imagination. Poets have praised its perfect beauty. Painters have striven to render its essence in oil, pastel, and watercolor. Architects have incorporated its image into soaring cathedrals, and folk have used it to decorate lavish mansions and humble cottages alike. Magicians and herbalists number this favorite flower among their agents of enchantment and healing.

We grow roses in our gardens, arrange them by the vaseful in our homes, and splash their pictures on slipcovers and draperies, carpets and linens. We wear the essence of the rose as perfume, preserve its sweet scent in potpourri, bathe in rose-scented waters, light rose-scented candles, even dine on confections flavored with roses.

Where did roses come from? In actuality, this most regal of blossoms began as a simple, five-petaled wildflower. Thousands of years of cultivation and breeding have transformed it into the sumptuous, elegant garden flower we know today.

The rose is the most universally beloved of all flowers, and has been in cultivation for millennia. Roses have been grown in China since about 2700 B.C., and they grew in the gardens of the Egyptian pharaohs and the Roman emperors as well. The crusaders brought damask roses to Europe when they returned from the wars in the Middle East; then Europeans, too, fell under the spell of the rose, and took up its growing and hybridizing. In the early 1800s the Empress Josephine established the first—and largest—modern-style collection of roses in her gardens at Malmaison. The gardens contained more than two hundred varieties of roses, and she commissioned the noted botanical illustrator Pierre-Joseph Redouté to paint their portraits.

From Europe the rose traveled to the New World with the colonists, who found that Native Americans already liked to plant wild roses around their campsites. In fact, roses had been growing in North America far earlier—fossilized remains of roses forty million years old have been found in Colorado.

The origin of the rose dwells also in the realm of myth and legend. Tales told in medieval Europe held that a white rose bloomed in the first garden on Earth—the garden of Eden. When Eve kissed it the flower blushed, and the first pink rose was born. The Romans believed that Bacchus, the god of wine, created the pink rose. The first red rose, they said, came from the love goddess Venus, and was colored with a few drops of her blood.

According to another myth, when Venus, fully formed, rose from the sea on her scallop shell, Earth was filled with jealousy and resolved to create something just as lovely. The rose—perfect in form and exquisitely fragrant—was the result.

The ancient Greeks had a different story. According to legend, Chloris, the goddess of flowers, was out walking on an errand one day when she found the body of a beautiful nymph who had been killed by bee stings. She took the nymph's body to Mount Olympus and asked the other gods to help turn her into a new flower. Aphrodite gave the flower beauty, Dionysus gave it nectar and fragrance, and the Three Graces bestowed joy, charm, and brilliance. From his chariot in the sky, Apollo, the sun god, sent a warming blush. Thus the rose was born.

To poets through the ages the rose has been a symbol of beauty and romantic love. More than four thousand published songs include references to roses. Shakespeare wrote often of the rose, and Robert Burns compared his beloved to a red rose. The Victorians were besotted with the stunning blooms, and in the language of flowers in use at the time, roses were assigned several different meanings. The red rose, especially a cabbage rose, spoke of love. A yellow rose indicated jealousy and a fading of love. The white rose said, "I am worthy of you," while a white rosebud stood for innocence. China roses meant beauty that is always new.

Architects, too, have turned to the rose, using it to ornament buildings. In the twelfth century, European cathedrals were adorned with spectacular round stained glass windows in the form of a rose. Rose motifs were carved into the ceilings, and above confessionals, where they came to symbolize secrecy. The phrase *sub rosa* ("under the rose"), which still refers to something told in confidence and not to be repeated, originated there.

To herbalists and magicians, the rose has ritual and magic powers. Believers have, for example, used roses for protection from evil influences. One could fashion a wreath of herbs, roses, and other flowers to hang on the front door or over the hearth. To keep unwanted trespassers away from a garden of herbs used for making magic, plant three red roses (or other red flowers) there. For sweet dreams, sleep on a pillow stuffed with rose petals, lemon balm, mint, costmary, and cloves.

Above all, the rose is the flower of love. Oil distilled from roses has been used in all sorts of love charms and potions. A blend of the oils of rose, lavender, jasmine, musk, and ylang-ylang was said to be so powerful it made a woman who wore it irresistibly attractive to men.

Long ago in England, a girl could scatter rose petals over the ground on Midsummer's Eve in the moonlight. If at the stroke of midnight she recited a special incantation, she would turn around to see a vision of the man she was to marry. In Persia, a girl could bring back a straying lover by boiling his shirt in rosewater and spices.

The beautiful and much-traveled rose still captures our hearts, and today remains a favorite of gardeners the world over. With its regal form, ravishing fragrance, and rich palette of heart-warming colors, the rose is surely the queen of all flowers.

— Anne Halpin

The wilderness and the solitary place

shall be glad for them;

and the desert shall rejoice and blossom

as the rose.

Isaiah

Would Jove a Queen of Flowers ordain,

The Rose, the Queen of Flowers should reign.

The Grace of Plants! the Pride of bowers,

The blush of Meads, the eye of flowers,

Her sweets the breath of love disclose,

Cythera's favorite bloom she glows.

What flower is half so lovely found,

As when, with full-blown beauties crowned,

The Rose each ravished sense beguiles

And on soft amorous Zephyr smiles?

Sappho, "Ode to the Rose"

Tis the last rose of summer,

Left blooming alone;

All her lovely companions

Are faded and gone;

No flower of her kindred

No rose-bud is nigh,

To reflect back her blushes,

Or give sigh for sigh.

Thomas Moore, "The Last Rose of Summer"

Roses at first were white,
Till they co'd not agree
Whether my Sappho's breast
Or they more white sho'd be.

But being vanquisht quite,
A blush their cheeks bespread:
Since which (believe the rest)
The Roses first came red.

Robert Herrick, "How Roses Came Red"

There's a bower of roses by Bendemeer's stream

And the nightingale sings 'round it all the day long:

In the times of my childhood 'twas like a sweet dream

To sit 'mid the roses and hear the bird's song.

"Bendemeer's Stream," folk song

. . . For us the rose from year to year renews in abundance

The yellow stamens of its crimson flower.

Far and away the best of all in power and fragrance,

It well deserves its name "the Flower of Flowers."

It colors the oil which bears its name. No man can say,

No man remembers, how many uses there are

For Oil of Roses as a cure for mankind's ailments.

Over against it grows the famous lily:

Its flowers breathe a scent which hangs

Long in the air; but he who crushes the gleaming buds

Of its snow-white flowers will find to his amazement

That the heavenly perfume, sweet as a scattering of nectar,

Vanishes in a moment.

Walafrid Strabo, *Hortulus*

Nor did I wonder at the lily's white

Nor praise the deep vermilion of the Rose:

They were but sweet, but figures of delight,

Drawn after you, you pattern of all those.

Yet seemed it winter still, and you away,

As with your shadow I with those did play.

William Shakespeare, *A Midsummer Night's Dream*

Roses white and red bloomed upon the spray:

One opened, leaf by leaf, to greet the morn,

Shyly at first, then in sweet disarray;

Another, yet a youngling, newly born,

Scarce struggled from the bud.

Lorenzo de' Medici

The true gardener, fickle lover that he is, should grow as many roses as he can find space for, that he may wander as the mood will take him, here and there from rose to rose, and in happy moments of imagination feast on a very nectar and ambrosia of scent and vision, and take his fill of happiness.

M. Waterfield, *Flower Grouping*

A charming paradisiacal mingling of all that was pleasant to the eyes and good for food....You gathered a Moss Rose one moment and a bunch of currants the next; you were in a delicious fluctuation between the scent of Jasmine and the juice of Gooseberries; the crimson of a Carnation was carried out in the lurking of the neighboring Strawberry Beds.

George Eliot

The rose is a rose,

And was always a rose,

But the theory now goes

That the apple's a rose,

And the pear is, and so's

The plum, I suppose.

The dear only knows

What will next prove a rose.

You, of course, are a rose—

But were always a rose.

Robert Frost, "Rose Family"

Oh, little rose tree, bloom!

Summer is nearly over.

The dahlias bleed, and the phlox is seed.

Nothing's left of the clover.

And the path of the poppy no one knows.

I would blossom if I were a rose.

Edna St. Vincent Millay

Who, that was blessed with parents that indulged

themselves, and children with a flower garden,

can forget the happy innocent hours spent in its cultivation!

O! who can forget those days, when to announce

the appearance of a bud, or the coloring of a tulip,

or the opening of a rose, or the perfection of a

full-blown peony, was glory enough for one morning.

Joseph Breck, *New Book of Flowers*

"*Our highest assurance of the goodness of Providence,*" *Holmes speculated,* "*seems to me to rest in the flowers. All other things, our desires, our food, are really necessary for our existence in the first instance. But this rose is an extra. Its smell and its colour are an embellishment of life, not a condition of it. It is only goodness which gives extras, and so I say again that we have much to hope for from the flowers.*"

Sir Arthur Conan Doyle, *The Memoirs of Sherlock Holmes*

Mine is the month of Roses; yes and mine

The month of Marriages! All pleasant sights

And scents, the fragrance of the blossoming vine,

The foliage of the valleys and the heights.

Mine are the longest days, the loveliest nights;

The mower's scythe makes music to my ear;

I am the mother of all dear delights;

I am the fairest daughter of the year.

Henry Wadsworth Longfellow, "The Poet's Calendar"

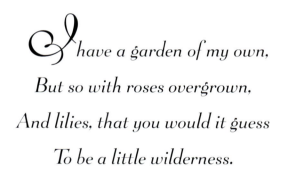

I have a garden of my own,

But so with roses overgrown,

And lilies, that you would it guess

To be a little wilderness.

Andrew Marvell, "The Nymph Complaining for the Death of Her Fawn"

The roses: their richness, variety, etc., will no doubt

always make them necessary to the poets.

Gerard Manley Hopkins

Oh, tell me how my garden grows,
Now I no more may labor there;
Do still the lily and the rose
Bloom on without my fostering care?

Mildred Howells

The rose spoke of burning loves, the lily of her chaste delight; the superb magnolia told of pure enjoyment and lofty pride; and the lovely little hepatica related the pleasure of a simple and returned existence.

George Sand, *Consuelo*

The rose bushes were planted along the sides of the road which ran through our village and were greatly admired by the passersby, but it was strongly impressed on us that a rose was useful, not ornamental. It was not intended to please us by its color or its odor. Its mission was to be made into rosewater, and if we thought of it in any other way we were making an idol of it and thereby imperilling our souls.

A sister in a Shaker community

Loveliest of lovely things are they,

On earth, that soonest pass away.

The rose that lives its little hour

Is prized beyond the sculptured flower.

William Cullen Bryant

The cowslip is a country wench,

The violet is a nun;—

But I will woo the dainty rose,

The queen of every one.

Thomas Hood

Roses, ye glowing ones,

Balsam—bestowing ones!

Fluttering, quivering,

Sweetness delivering.

Branching unblightedly,

Budding delightedly,

Bloom and be seen!

Springtime declare him,

In purple and green!

Paradise bear him,

The Sleeper serene!

Johann Wolfgang von Goethe, *Faust*

You for Antiquity, rose throned in power,

were a calyx with only a single rim,

but for us of to-day you're the full, the numberless flower,

the theme whose depths we can only skim.

Grown so rich, you appear like draping on draping

about a body of air and fire;

though each of your leaves in itself is at once an escaping

and a disowning of all attire.

For centuries, name, after sweetest name,

we have heard your fragrance singing:

suddenly it hangs in the air like fame.

And then we find no name, it exceeds our powers...

and over to it go winging

memories yielded up by recallable hours.

Rainer Maria Rilke

Ye violets that first appear,

By your pure purple mantles known,

Like the proud virgins of the year,

As if the spring were all your own,

What are you when the Rose is blown?

Sir Henry Wotton

In my Autumn garden I was fain

To mourn among my scattered roses;

Alas for that last rosebud that uncloses

To Autumn's languid sun and rain

When all the world is on the wain!

Which has not felt the sweet constraint of June,

Nor heard the nightingale in tune.

Broad-faced asters by my garden walk,

You are but coarse compared with roses:

More choice, more dear that rosebud which uncloses,

Faint-scented, pinched, upon its stalk,

That least and last which cold winds balk;

A rose it is though least and last of all,

A rose to me though at the fall.

Christina Rossetti, "October Garden"

You love the roses—so do I. I wish
The sky would rain down roses, as they rain
From off the shaken bush. Why will it not?
Then all the valley would be pink and white
And soft to tread on. They would fall as light
As feathers, smelling sweet: and it would be
Like sleeping and yet waking, all at once.

George Eliot

"My little plot," said Miss Mapp. "Very modest, as you see, three quarters of an acre at the most, but well screened. My flower beds: sweet roses, tortoiseshell butterflies. Rather a nice clematis: My little Eden, I call it, so small, but so well loved."

E. F. Benson

See how the flowers, as at parade,

Under their colours stand display'd:

Each regiment in order grows, that of the tulip, pink, and rose.

Andrew Marvell

The morning rose that untouch'd stands

Arm'd with her briers, how sweet she smells!

But pluck'd and strain'd through ruder hands,

Her sweets no longer with her dwells.

Sir Robert Aytoun

The rose has one powerful virtue to boast

Above all the flowers of the field:

When its leaves are all dead, and fine colours are lost,

Still how sweet a perfume

It will yield!

Isaac Watts

If love were what the rose is,
And I were like the leaf,
Our lives would grow together
In sad or singing weather.

Algernon Charles Swinburne, "A Match"

You can't forget a garden

When you have planted seed—

When you have watched the weather

And know a rose's need.

Louise Driscoll

This morning we pulled ourselves together and went to a little village about thirty minutes away by bus, l'Hay des Roses, and walked through an immense rose garden just coming into bloom. Oh, at least a million roses, far too many, really. I should prefer about half an acre, with a dozen varieties very carefully chosen and tended. Some of those heavy dark red roses we used to have, some fine shell-pink-beige tea roses, Gold of Phir, Gloire de Dijon, several climbing kinds, and a hedge or two of wild roses, and the whole thing surrounded by a carefully clipped wall of cape jessamines. I can see it, I know just how it should look. Some day I may even have it.

Katherine Anne Porter

Jasmine is all in white and has many loves,

And the broom's betrothed to the bee;

But I will plight with the dainty rose,

For fairest of all is she.

Thomas Hood

"I haven't much time to be fond of anything," says Sergeant Cuff. "But when I have a moment's fondness to bestow, most times...the roses get it."

Wilkie Collins, *The Moonstone*

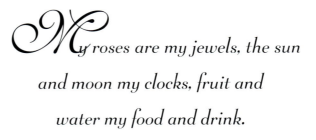

My roses are my jewels, the sun and moon my clocks, fruit and water my food and drink.

Hester Lucy Stanhope

Preparing a bed for roses is a little like getting the house ready for the arrival of a difficult old lady, some biddy with aristocratic pretensions and persnickety tastes. Her stay is bound to be an ordeal, and you want to give her as little cause for complaint as possible.

Michael Pollan

I know a little garden close,

Set thick with lily and with rose,

Where I would wander if I might

From dewy dawn to dewy night.

William Morris

The serene philosophy of the pink rose is steadying. Its fragrant, delicate petals open fully and are ready to fall, without regret or disillusion, after only a day in the sun. It is so every summer. One can almost hear their pink, fragrant murmur as they settle down upon the grass: "Summer, summer, it will always be summer."

Rachel Peden

The red rose whispers of passion,

And the white rose breathes of love;

O, the red rose is a falcon,

And the white rose is a dove.

But I send you a cream-white rosebud

With a flush on its petal tips;

For the love that is purest and sweetest

Has a kiss of desire on the lips.

John Boyle O'Reilly, "A White Rose"

Gather therefore the Rose, whilst yet is

prime,

For soon comes age, that will her pride de-

flower:

Gather the Rose of love, whilst yet is time.

Edmund Spenser, *The Faerie Queene*

Dead-heading the roses on a summer evening is an occupation to carry us back into a calmer age and a different century. Queen Victoria might still be on the throne. All is quiet in the garden: the paths are pale: our silent satellite steals up the sky: even the aeroplanes have gone to roost and our own nerves have ceased to twangle. There is no sound except the hoot of an howl, and the rhythmic snip-snap of our own secateurs, cutting the dead heads off, back to a new bud, to provoke new growth for the immediate future.

Vita Sackville-West

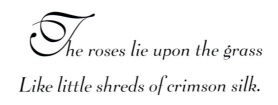

The roses lie upon the grass
Like little shreds of crimson silk.

Oscar Wilde

O, how much more doth beauty beauteous seem

By that sweet ornament which truth doth give!

The rose looks fair, but fairer we it deem

For that sweet odour which doth in it live.

The canker-blooms have full as deep a dye

As the perfumed tincture of the roses,

Hang on such thorns and play as wantonly

When summer's breath their masked buds discloses:

But, for their virtue only is their show,

They live unwoo'd and unrespected fade,

Die to themselves. Sweet roses do not so;

Of their sweet deaths are sweetest odours made:

And so of you, beauteous and lovely youth,

When that shall fade, my verse distills your truth.

William Shakespeare, Sonnet LIV

Queen rose of the rosebud garden of girls,
Come hither, the dances are done,
In gloss of satin and glimmer of pearls,
Queen lily and rose in one;
Shine out, little head, sunning over with curls,
To the flowers, and be their sun.

Alfred, Lord Tennyson, *Maud*

Why must I think how oft we two

Have sate together near the river springs....

While the musk-rose leaves, like flakes of crimson snow

Showered upon us, and the dove mourned in the pine

Sad prophetess of sorrows not our own.

Percy Bysshe Shelley

Margaret was buried in the lower chancel

and William in the higher;

Out of her breast there sprang a rose

And out of his a briar.

They grew till they grew up to the church top,

And then they could grow no higher;

And there they tied in a true lover's knot

The red rose and the briar.

"Fair Margaret and Sweet William," folk song

As late I rambled in the happy fields,

What time the sky-lark shakes the tremulous dew

From his lush clover covert;—when anew

Adventurous knights take up their dinted shields:

I saw the sweetest flower wild nature yields,

A fresh-blown musk-rose; 'twas the first that threw

Its sweets upon the summer; graceful it grew

As is the wand that queen Titania wields.

And, as I feasted on its fragrancy,

I thought the garden-rose it far excell'd:

But when, O Wells! thy roses came to me

My sense with their deliciousness was spell'd:

Soft voices have they, that with tender plea

Whisper'd of peace, and truth, and friendliness unquell'd.

John Keats

And the rose like a nymph to the bath addrest,

Which unveiled the depth of her glowing breast,

Till, fold after fold, to the fainting air

The soul of her beauty and love lay bare...

Percy Bysshe Shelley

The rose was dedicated to the goddess of love, that is, to the eternal mystery of the continuity of life. As such it was the symbol of mystery and secrecy. "Mystery glows in the rose bed, the secret is hidden in the rose," sang the Persian poet and perfumer, Farid ud-din Attar, in the twelfth century. A more prosaic explanation is that the folded structure of the rose, by its nature, conceals a secret inner core.

Gabriele Tergit, *Flowers Through the Ages*

The simple fact is that anyone can grow a rose
if he has a kind heart, and as the nursing books advocate,
shows a little sympathy with the patient. It is just a
case of doing as one would be done by.

Ethelind Fearon

Like a rose embowered

In its own green leaves,

By warm winds deflowered,

Till the scent it gives

Makes faint with too much sweet

These heavy-winged thieves.

Percy Bysshe Shelley, "To a Skylark"

Sweet is the rose, but grows upon a brere;

Sweet is the Junipere, but sharp his bough;

Sweet is the Eglantine, but pricketh nere;

Sweet is the Firbloom, but his branches rough;

Sweet is the Cypresse, but his rynd is tough;

Sweet is the nut, but bitter is his pill;

Sweet is the Broom-flower, but yet sowre enough;

And sweet is Moly, but his root is ill.

So every sweet with soure is tempered still,

That maketh it be coveted the more:

For easie things, that may be got at will,

Most sorts of men doe set but little store.

Edmund Spenser

The little space which scented box encloses

Is blue with lupins and is sweet with thyme

My garden all is overblown with roses,

My spirit all is overblown with rhyme,

As like a drunken honeybee I waver

From house to garden and again to house,

And, undetermined which delight to favour,

On verse and rose alternatively carouse.

Vita Sackville-West

Lancasters wore the red, red rose,
And all of York the white,
And England plunged in bloody wars
To find out which was right.

Thus rose became the right and badge
Of lineage and kings,
Established as the queen of flowers
Of which the poet sings.

It furnished emblems without end,
As at a death, each tear
Is gently wiped away by a rose
As it falls upon the bier.

Joshua Freeman Crowell

A garden is a lovesome thing, God wot!

Rose plot, fringed pool, ferned grot—

The veriest school

Of peace, and yet the fool

Contends that God is not—

Not God! In gardens when the eve is cool?

Nay, but I have a sign,

'Tis very sure God walks in mine.

Thomas Edward Brown

The single rose is, in essence, a symbol of completion, of consummate achievement and perfection. Hence, accruing to it are all those ideas associated with these qualities: the mystic Centre, the heart, the garden of Eros, the paradise of Dante, the Beloved, the emblem of Venus.

J. E. Cirlot, *A Dictionary of Symbols*

Leave not the business of today to be done

tomorrow....The rose garden which today is full

of flowers, tomorrow, when thou wouldst pluck

a rose, may not afford thee even one.

Firdawsi

Roses—nothing can be more favourable than to
dream of these beautiful flowers, as they are certain emblems
of happiness, prosperity, and long life.

A Victorian Book of Dreams

It was the sweetest, most mysterious-looking place anyone could imagine. The high walls which shut it in were covered with the leafless stems of climbing roses, which were so thick that they were matted together....All the ground was covered with grass of a wintry brown, and out of it grew clumps of bushes which were surely rose-bushes if they were alive. There were numbers of standard roses which had so spread their branches that they were like little trees. There were other trees in the garden, and one of the things which made the place look strangest and loveliest was that climbing roses had run all over them and swung down long tendrils which made light swaying curtains, and here and there they had caught at each other or at a far-reaching branch and had crept from one tree to another and made lovely bridges of themselves.

Frances Hodgson Burnett, *The Secret Garden*

Soon will set in the fitful weather, with fierce gales

and sullen skies and frosty air, and it will be time to

tuck up safely my Roses and Lilies and the rest for

their winter sleep beneath the snow, where

I never forget them, but ever dream of their

wakening in happy summers yet to be.

Celia Thaxter

And in the warm hedge grew lush eglantine,

Green cowbird and the moonlight-coloured May,

And cherry blossoms, and white cups, whose wine

Was the bright dew, yet drained not by the day;

And wild roses and ivy serpentine,

With its dark buds and leaves wandering astray;

And flowers azure, black, and streaked with gold,

Fairer than any weakened eyes behold.

Percy Bysshe Shelley, "The Question"

Perhaps few people have ever asked themselves why they admire a rose so much more than all other flowers. If they consider, they will find, first that red is, in a delicately graduated state, the loveliest of all pure colors; and secondly, that in the rose there is no shadow, except which is composed of color. All its shadows are fuller in color than its lights, owing to the translucency and reflective power of its leaves.

John Ruskin

What's in a name? That which we call a

rose

By any other name would smell as sweet.

William Shakespeare, *Romeo and Juliet*

Go, lovely rose!

Tell her that wastes her time and me

That now she knows,

When I resemble her to thee,

How sweet and fair she seems to be.

Edmund Waller, "Go, Lovely Rose"

*Into the yellow anthers of the rose eternal—the rose
that expands by degrees and yields perfumes in praise
of the sun, the source of eternal spring—Beatrice,
silent, though wanting to speak, drew me...*

Dante Alighieri, *The Divine Comedy*

Chill'd by the night, the drooping

Rose of May

Mourns the long absence of the

lovely Day;

Young Day returning at her

promis'd hour

Weeps o'er the sorrows of her

favourite Flower.

Samuel Taylor Coleridge, "The Hour When We Shall Meet Again"

A floral symbol sacred to Venus and signifying love, the quality and nature of which was characterized by the color of the rose. A symbol of purity, a white rose represented innocent (nonsexual) love, while a pink rose represented first love, and a red rose true love.

The Dictionary of Christian Art

Spirits! to you the infant Maid was given

Form'd by the wond'rous Alchemy of Heaven!

No fairer Maid does Love's wide empire know,

No fairer Maid e'er heav'd the bosom's snow.

A thousand Loves around her forehead fly;

A thousand Loves sit melting in her eye;

Love lights her smile—in Joy's red nectar dips

The flamy rose, and plants it on her lips!

Samuel Taylor Coleridge, "Lines on an Autumnal Evening"

It happened that where the Prince's father lay buried,
there grew a rose tree—a most beautiful rose tree which
blossomed only once in five years, and even then it bore
only one flower, but that was a rose.
It smelt so sweet that all cares and sorrows were
forgotten by him who inhaled its fragrance.

Hans Christian Andersen

The Rose is the honour and beauty of flowers,

The Rose is the care and love of the Spring,

The Rose is the pleasure of th' heavenly Pow'rs.

The Boy of Faire Venus, Cythera's Darling

Doth wrap his head round with Garlands of Rose

When in the dances of the Graces he goes.

Anacreon

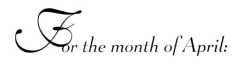

For the month of April:

Upon her head a cremosin coronet

With damaske roses and daffadillies set;

Bay leaves betweene, and primroses greene,

Embellish the sweete violet.

Edmund Spenser, "The Shepherd's Calendar"

Light splashed this morning

on the shell-pink anemones

swaying on their tall stems;

down blue-spiked veronica

light flowed in rivulets

over the humps of the honeybees;

this morning I saw light kiss

the silk on the roses

in their second flowering,

my late bloomers

flushed with their brandy.

A curious gladness shook me.

Stanley Kunitz, "The Round"

A large rose-tree stood near the entrance of the garden:

the roses growing on it were white, but

there were three gardeners at it, busily painting

them red. Alice thought this a very curious thing,

and she went nearer to watch them, and just as

she came up to them she heard one of them say,

"Look at that now, Five! Don't go splashing paint

over me like that!"

Lewis Carroll, *Alice's Adventures in Wonderland*

With the year

Seasons return, but not to me returns

Day or the sweet approach of ev'n or morn

Or sight of vernal bloom or summer's rose.

John Milton

And bid Arcadia bloom around:

Whether we fringe the sloping hill

Or smooth below the verdant mead,

Whether we break the falling rill,

Or through meandering mazes lead,

Or in the horrid bramble's room

Bid careless groups of roses bloom.

William Shenstone

Sweet Rose, whose hue angry and brave

Bids the rash gazer wipe his eye,

Thy root is ever in its grave,

And thou must die.

George Herbert

Strew on her roses, roses,

And never a spray of yew.

In quiet she reposes:

Ah! would that I did too.

Matthew Arnold

I cannot see what flowers are at my feet,

Nor what soft incense hangs upon the boughs,

but, in embalmed darkness, guess each sweet

Where with the seasonable month endows

The grass, the thicket, and the fruit-tree wild;

White hawthorn, and the pastoral eglantine;

Fast fading violets cover'd up in leaves;

And mid-May's eldest child,

The coming musk-rose, full of dewy wine,

The murmurous haunt of flies on summer eves.

John Keats, "Ode to a Nightingale"

I sent thee late a rosy wreath,

Not so much honoring thee,

As giving it a hope, that there

It could not withered be.

But thou thereon did'st only breathe.

And sent'st it back to me;

Since when it grows and smells, I swear,

Not of itself but thee.

Ben Jonson, "Song, To Celia"

He who would have beautiful roses in his garden

must have beautiful roses in his heart.

Dean Hole

Hail and flourish, rejoice and be strong

O Mary, no springtime wreath of rosebuds do I entwine

But, for you, from the roses, a spiritual one.

Saint Bernard, saying the rosary

Ask me no more where Jove bestows,

When June is past, the fading rose:

For in your beauty's orient deep

These flowers, as in their causes, sleep.

Thomas Carew, "To Celia"

Poetry is lavish of roses; it heaps them into beds,

weaves them into crowns, twines them with the goblet used

in the festivals of Bacchus, plants them in the bosom of

beauty—nay, not only delights in the rose itself upon

every occasion, but seizes each particular beauty it

possesses as an object of comparison to the loveliest works

of nature—as soft as a rose-leaf; as sweet as a rose; rosy

clouds; rosy cheeks; rosy lips; rosy blushes; rosy dawns...

Joseph Breck, *The Flower Garden,*

My lady's presence makes the roses red,

Because to see her lips they blush for shame:

The lily's leaves, for envy, pale became,

And her white hands in them this envy bred.

The marigold abroad her leaves doth spred,

Because the sun's and her power is the same;

The violet of purple colour came,

Dyed with the blood she made my heart to shed.

In brief, all flowers from her their virtue take:

From her sweet breath their sweet smells do proceed,

The living heat which her eye-beams do make

Warmeth the ground, and quickeneth the seed.

The rain wherewith she watereth these flowers

Falls from mine eyes, which she dissolves in showers.

Henry Constable, "Of His Mistress, upon Occasion of Her Walking in a Garden"

There is a garden in her face,

Where roses and white lilies grow,

A heavenly paradise is that place,

Wherein all pleasant fruits do flow.

Thomas Campion

Rememberest thou, from long ago,
The wondrous gold of Ophir's glow?

Is fragrance your despairing sigh
Because the sun smites you and you die?

Dear flower, I'll whisper, ere you go,
Why, all my life, I've loved you so.

I dreamed that beauty, ere she fled,
For your fair dower her mantle shed!

Joshua Freeman Crowell, "Yellow Rose, Garden Wise and Otherwise"

Love, thou art fair, as delicate as dew

Upon a rose-leaf thy young freshness is.

O Love, the very perfume of the rose,

As the dew carries it about the sward,

Smiting my senses like an unseen sword,

Out from the rose-bush of your bosom blows;

And lo! the very nightingales are mad,

Frenzied with singing—just as though they had

Looked one delirious moment in your face.

Now that the rose-tree in its dainty hand

Lifts high its brimming cup of blood-red wine,

And green buds thicken o'er the empty land,

Heart, leave these speculations deep of thine,

And seek the grassy wilderness with me.

Who cares for problems, human or divine!

Hafiz

Are we energumens, or the tropics, or mad Provence, to hope that here where we live, January will bring the bloom to the Rose? But I see that we are sufficiently intoxicated by it for me to grant its name a capital R; all the more because the last war priced it like gold.... The shop was resplendent with those roses that have lips, cheeks, breasts, navels, flesh glistening with an indescribable frost; roses that travel by air, stand erect on the end of a disdainful stem, and smell of peaches, tea, and even of roses....Unattainable roses. Rose, wherein are your former lovers satisfied? Like all lovers aged or dethroned, they content themselves with singing your praises. They gaze at you longingly, through the shop window. They sigh, they can describe you in covetous detail, they talk about your shape, about the tight whorl your hybrid nature requires. I think that, like me, they miss the blessed days of your imperfection.

Colette, *Rose, Flowers and Fruit*

And after all the weather was ideal! They could not have had a more perfect day for a garden-party if they had ordered it. Windless, warm, the sky without a cloud. Only the blue was veiled with a haze of light gold, as it is sometimes in early summer. The gardener had been up since dawn, mowing the lawns and sweeping them, until the grass and the dark flat rosettes where the daisy plants had been seemed to shine. As for the roses, you could not help feeling they understood that roses are the only flowers that impress people at garden parties; the only flowers that everyone is certain of knowing. Hundreds, yes, literally hundreds, had come out in a single night; the green bushes bowed down as if they had been visited by archangels.

Katherine Mansfield

I have to go to my roses, which never seem to be more beautiful than at sunrise, when the dew drops are still sparkling on the petals. What a fragrance and symphony of color in the stillness of dawn.

Lotte Gunthart, *A Day with the Rose*

Now, did I not so near my labours end,

Strike sail, and hastening to the harbour tend,

My song of flower gardens might extend

To teach the vegetable arts, to sing

The Paestan roses, and their double spring.

Virgil, *Georgics*

Very old are the woods;

And the buds that break

Out of that briar's boughs,

When March winds wake,

So old with their beauty are—

Oh no man knows

Through what wild centuries

Rose back the rose.

Walter de la Mare

His eye lit on a cluster of yellow roses. He had never seen any as sun-golden before, and his first impulse was to send them to May instead of the lilies. But they did not look like her—there was something too rich, too strong, in their fiery beauty.

Edith Wharton, *Age of Innocence*

I don't know whether nice people tend to grow roses or growing roses makes people nice.

Roland A. Browne

IDENTIFICATION GUIDE TO THE ROSES

PHOTOGRAPHY CREDITS